EMMANUEL JOSEPH

The Astronomer's Diary, Bridging Literature, Psychology, and the Wonders of Space

Copyright © 2025 by Emmanuel Joseph

All rights reserved. No part of this publication may be reproduced, stored or transmitted in any form or by any means, electronic, mechanical, photocopying, recording, scanning, or otherwise without written permission from the publisher. It is illegal to copy this book, post it to a website, or distribute it by any other means without permission.

First edition

This book was professionally typeset on Reedsy. Find out more at reedsy.com

Contents

1. Chapter 1: The Dawn of Discovery ... 1
2. Chapter 2: A Universe of Stories ... 3
3. Chapter 3: Celestial Psyche ... 5
4. Chapter 4: The Literature of the Stars ... 7
5. Chapter 5: The Cosmic Dance ... 9
6. Chapter 6: The Psychology of Space ... 11
7. Chapter 7: The Literature of the Stars ... 13
8. Chapter 8: Celestial Synchronicity ... 15
9. Chapter 9: The Art of the Cosmos ... 17
10. Chapter 10: The Philosophy of the Stars ... 19
11. Chapter 11: The Intersection of Science and Spirituality ... 21
12. Chapter 12: The Legacy of the Stars ... 23
13. Epilogue: A New Dawn ... 25
14. Chapter 13: The Rhythms of the Cosmos ... 27
15. Chapter 14: The Universe Within ... 29
16. Chapter 15: The Future of Exploration ... 31

1

Chapter 1: The Dawn of Discovery

In the quiet town of Blue Haven, nestled beneath the vast, starry skies, Dr. Lydia Marlow found solace. She was a renowned astronomer, known for her insatiable curiosity and unique perspective on the universe. Her diary, a treasure trove of thoughts and observations, served as the foundation for an extraordinary journey that would bridge literature, psychology, and the wonders of space. In her writings, she often intertwined the poetic elegance of the cosmos with the intricate workings of the human mind. Through these reflections, Lydia sought to understand not just the universe, but the very essence of humanity.

The journey began with a single, transformative moment. One evening, while gazing through her telescope, Lydia witnessed a rare celestial event—a supernova exploding in a distant galaxy. This spectacle of cosmic beauty ignited a spark within her, compelling her to delve deeper into the mysteries of the universe. She pondered the parallels between the life cycle of stars and the human experience, drawing connections that would shape her life's work. Her diary became a canvas for these musings, a place where she could explore the profound interplay between the cosmos and the psyche.

As Lydia's fascination grew, so did her desire to share her insights with the world. She began incorporating literary references into her observations, drawing inspiration from the works of poets and philosophers who had also marveled at the night sky. Through their words, she found new ways to articulate the wonder and awe that the cosmos inspired. Her diary entries became a blend of scientific exploration and literary reverie, each page a testament to the beauty and complexity of the universe.

Lydia's work did not go unnoticed. Her unique approach to astronomy garnered the attention of both her peers and the public. She was invited to speak at conferences and symposiums, where she captivated audiences with her eloquent storytelling and profound insights. Through her diary, Lydia not only advanced the field of astronomy but also opened new pathways for understanding the human condition. Her journey had only just begun, but it was clear that she was destined to leave an indelible mark on the world.

2

Chapter 2: A Universe of Stories

Lydia's diary continued to evolve as she embarked on new adventures in her quest to unravel the mysteries of the universe. Each entry was a tapestry of scientific discovery and literary inspiration, weaving together the threads of her diverse interests. She found herself drawn to the stories of the stars, seeing them as not just celestial objects, but as characters in a grand cosmic narrative. Through her diary, she gave voice to these stories, crafting tales that resonated with the human experience.

One evening, while observing a distant nebula, Lydia was struck by its resemblance to a piece of classical art. She began to explore the connections between astronomy and visual storytelling, delving into the works of artists who had been inspired by the night sky. Her diary entries from this period are rich with descriptions of celestial wonders and their artistic counterparts, revealing the deep connections between science and creativity. Lydia's fascination with these intersections fueled her passion for sharing the beauty of the universe with others.

As she delved deeper into the world of literature, Lydia discovered the power of metaphor in understanding the cosmos. She saw parallels between the journeys of literary heroes and the paths of celestial bodies, each navigating their own unique challenges and transformations. Her diary became a reflection of these insights, filled with metaphors that bridged the gap between the tangible and the intangible. Lydia's writing was a testament to the power of language in illuminating the mysteries of the universe.

Lydia's diary was not just a personal record of her thoughts and discoveries; it was a bridge between worlds. Through her writing, she sought to connect the realms of science, literature, and psychology, creating a holistic understanding of the cosmos and the human mind. Her work inspired others to see the universe through new eyes, fostering a sense of wonder and curiosity that transcended disciplinary boundaries. Lydia's diary was a living testament to the endless possibilities of exploration and discovery.

3

Chapter 3: Celestial Psyche

Lydia's fascination with the cosmos extended beyond the physical realm; she was equally intrigued by the psychological implications of space exploration. She began to explore the ways in which the universe influenced human thought and behavior, delving into the emerging field of astropsychology. Her diary entries from this period are a blend of scientific inquiry and introspective reflection, revealing the profound impact of the cosmos on the human psyche.

One of Lydia's most significant insights came from her study of the moon's influence on human emotions. She observed the ways in which lunar cycles affected mood and behavior, drawing connections between the phases of the moon and the rhythms of daily life. Her diary became a repository of these observations, filled with detailed notes and reflections on the interplay between celestial events and psychological well-being. Lydia's work in this area opened new pathways for understanding the connections between the cosmos and the mind.

Lydia's exploration of astropsychology also led her to consider the impact of space travel on mental health. She delved into the experiences of astronauts, examining the psychological challenges they faced during their journeys. Her diary entries from this period are a testament to her empathy and insight, as she sought to understand the unique pressures of space travel and the ways in which the human mind adapted to these extreme conditions. Through her writing, Lydia highlighted the importance of psychological support for those who ventured into the cosmos.

Lydia's work in astropsychology was groundbreaking, paving the way for new research and understanding in the field. Her diary served as a catalyst for this exploration, providing a space for her to document her findings and share her insights with others. Through her writing, Lydia not only advanced the field of astronomy but also contributed to the growing body of knowledge on the psychological implications of space exploration. Her diary was a testament to the interconnectedness of the cosmos and the human mind.

4

Chapter 4: The Literature of the Stars

As Lydia's journey continued, she found herself increasingly drawn to the literary aspects of her work. She began to explore the ways in which literature and astronomy intersected, delving into the writings of poets and authors who had been inspired by the night sky. Her diary entries from this period are a blend of literary analysis and scientific observation, revealing the deep connections between the cosmos and the written word.

Lydia's exploration of literary astronomy led her to discover the works of poets such as Walt Whitman and John Keats, who had used the night sky as a source of inspiration for their poetry. She marveled at the ways in which these writers captured the beauty and mystery of the cosmos, using language to convey the awe and wonder of the universe. Her diary became a reflection of these insights, filled with poetic passages and literary references that bridged the gap between science and art.

Through her study of literary astronomy, Lydia also discovered the power of storytelling in understanding the cosmos. She saw the stars as characters in a grand cosmic narrative, each with their own unique stories to tell. Her diary entries from this period are rich with imaginative tales and metaphors, revealing the deep connections between the celestial and the terrestrial. Lydia's writing was a testament to the power of language in illuminating the mysteries of the universe.

Lydia's work in literary astronomy was a bridge between worlds, connecting the realms of science and literature in new and profound ways. Her diary served as a space for her to document her discoveries and share her insights with others, inspiring a sense of wonder and curiosity that transcended disciplinary boundaries. Through her writing, Lydia fostered a holistic understanding of the cosmos, one that celebrated the beauty and complexity of the universe and the written word.

5

Chapter 5: The Cosmic Dance

Lydia's journey through the cosmos was not just a solitary endeavor; it was a dance with the universe. She saw the stars and planets as partners in a grand cosmic ballet, each moving in harmony with the others. Her diary entries from this period are a reflection of this dance, filled with observations and reflections on the intricate movements of celestial bodies and the ways in which they mirrored the rhythms of life on Earth.

One of Lydia's most profound insights came from her study of the solar system's dance. She observed the ways in which the planets moved in their orbits, drawing connections between their motions and the cycles of human life. Her diary became a repository of these observations, filled with detailed notes and reflections on the interplay between celestial events and the rhythms of daily life. Lydia's work in this area opened new pathways for understanding the connections between the cosmos and the human experience.

Lydia's exploration of the cosmic dance also led her to consider the ways in which the universe influenced human creativity. She saw the stars as a source of inspiration for artists and musicians, drawing connections between the rhythms of the cosmos and the patterns of artistic expression. Her diary entries from this period are rich with descriptions of celestial wonders and their artistic counterparts, revealing the deep connections between science and creativity. Lydia's fascination with these intersections fueled her passion for sharing the beauty of the universe with others.

Lydia's work in the cosmic dance was a bridge between worlds, connecting the realms of science, art, and psychology in new and profound ways. Her diary served as a space for her to document her discoveries and share her insights with others, inspiring a sense of wonder and curiosity that transcended disciplinary boundaries. Through her writing, Lydia fostered a holistic understanding of the cosmos, one that celebrated the beauty and complexity of the universe and the human mind.

6

Chapter 6: The Psychology of Space

Lydia's fascination with the cosmos extended beyond the physical realm; she was equally intrigued by the psychological implications of space exploration. She began to explore the ways in which the universe influenced human thought and behavior, delving into the emerging field of astropsychology. Her diary entries from this period are a blend of scientific inquiry and introspective reflection, revealing the profound impact of the cosmos on the human psyche.

One of Lydia's most profound insights came from her study of isolation and confinement. She examined how prolonged periods in space, away from familiar surroundings and loved ones, affected mental health. Lydia's diary entries from this period are filled with empathetic reflections on the experiences of astronauts who faced the psychological challenges of space travel. She noted the importance of resilience, coping strategies, and support systems in maintaining mental well-being during extended missions. Her work shed light on the psychological demands of space exploration and the need for comprehensive mental health care for astronauts.

Lydia's exploration of astropsychology also led her to consider the impact of awe and wonder on the human mind. She observed how the vastness of the universe and the beauty of celestial phenomena inspired feelings of transcendence and connectedness. Her diary entries from this period are a testament to the power of the cosmos in evoking profound emotional responses. Lydia's insights highlighted the therapeutic potential of space-related experiences, suggesting that exposure to the wonders of the universe could foster a sense of awe and promote psychological well-being.

Through her research, Lydia also explored the concept of the "overview effect," a phenomenon experienced by astronauts when they view Earth from space. She documented the transformative impact of this perspective shift, noting how it fostered a sense of unity, interconnectedness, and responsibility towards the planet. Lydia's diary entries from this period are filled with thoughtful reflections on the implications of the overview effect for humanity. Her work contributed to a deeper understanding of how space exploration could influence human consciousness and inspire a greater sense of global stewardship.

Lydia's pioneering work in astropsychology bridged the gap between the cosmos and the human mind. Her diary served as a space for her to document her findings and share her insights, inspiring a new field of study that explored the psychological dimensions of space exploration. Through her writing, Lydia not only advanced the understanding of the universe but also deepened the knowledge of the human psyche. Her diary was a testament to the interconnectedness of the cosmos and the mind, and the profound impact of space on human thought and behavior.

7

Chapter 7: The Literature of the Stars

As Lydia's journey continued, she found herself increasingly drawn to the literary aspects of her work. She began to explore the ways in which literature and astronomy intersected, delving into the writings of poets and authors who had been inspired by the night sky. Her diary entries from this period are a blend of literary analysis and scientific observation, revealing the deep connections between the cosmos and the written word.

Lydia's exploration of literary astronomy led her to discover the works of poets such as Walt Whitman and John Keats, who had used the night sky as a source of inspiration for their poetry. She marveled at the ways in which these writers captured the beauty and mystery of the cosmos, using language to convey the awe and wonder of the universe. Her diary became a reflection of these insights, filled with poetic passages and literary references that bridged the gap between science and art.

Through her study of literary astronomy, Lydia also discovered the power of storytelling in understanding the cosmos. She saw the stars as characters in a grand cosmic narrative, each with their own unique stories to tell. Her diary entries from this period are rich with imaginative tales and metaphors, revealing the deep connections between the celestial and the terrestrial. Lydia's writing was a testament to the power of language in illuminating the mysteries of the universe.

Lydia's work in literary astronomy was a bridge between worlds, connecting the realms of science and literature in new and profound ways. Her diary served as a space for her to document her discoveries and share her insights with others, inspiring a sense of wonder and curiosity that transcended disciplinary boundaries. Through her writing, Lydia fostered a holistic understanding of the cosmos, one that celebrated the beauty and complexity of the universe and the written word.

8

Chapter 8: Celestial Synchronicity

Lydia's journey through the cosmos was marked by moments of synchronicity—instances where the movements of celestial bodies seemed to mirror the events of her own life. These moments of alignment between the macrocosm and the microcosm fascinated her, and she dedicated a significant portion of her diary to exploring these connections. Her entries from this period are filled with reflections on the ways in which the universe seemed to communicate with her, offering insights and guidance through its celestial dance.

One of Lydia's most profound experiences of celestial synchronicity occurred during a total solar eclipse. As the moon passed between the Earth and the sun, casting a shadow over the land, Lydia experienced a moment of deep introspection. She saw the eclipse as a metaphor for the cycles of darkness and light in her own life, drawing parallels between the celestial event and her personal journey. Her diary became a space for her to document these reflections, filled with poetic passages that captured the beauty and mystery of the eclipse.

Lydia also observed the ways in which planetary alignments influenced human behavior and events. She noted that certain configurations of planets seemed to coincide with significant moments in history, drawing connections between the movements of the cosmos and the unfolding of human events. Her diary entries from this period are a blend of astrological observation and historical analysis, revealing the deep connections between the celestial and the terrestrial. Lydia's work in this area opened new pathways for understanding the interplay between the cosmos and human affairs.

Through her exploration of celestial synchronicity, Lydia discovered the power of the cosmos to inspire a sense of wonder and connectedness. She saw the stars and planets as guides, offering insights and wisdom through their movements. Her diary became a repository of these reflections, filled with detailed notes and poetic passages that celebrated the beauty and complexity of the universe. Lydia's work in celestial synchronicity was a testament to the interconnectedness of all things, revealing the profound impact of the cosmos on the human experience.

Chapter 9: The Art of the Cosmos

Lydia's fascination with the cosmos extended beyond the realms of science and literature; she was also deeply intrigued by the artistic representations of the universe. She began to explore the ways in which artists had captured the beauty and mystery of the night sky, delving into the works of painters, sculptors, and photographers who had been inspired by the stars. Her diary entries from this period are rich with descriptions of celestial art, revealing the deep connections between science and creativity.

One of Lydia's most significant discoveries came from her study of Van Gogh's "Starry Night." She marveled at the ways in which the artist had captured the swirling patterns of the night sky, using color and texture to convey the awe and wonder of the cosmos. Her diary became a space for her to document her reflections on the painting, filled with detailed notes and poetic passages that celebrated the beauty and complexity of Van Gogh's work. Lydia's insights highlighted the power of art to evoke a sense of wonder and connectedness with the universe.

Lydia's exploration of celestial art also led her to consider the ways in which modern artists had captured the beauty of the cosmos. She delved into the works of contemporary photographers who had used advanced technology to capture stunning images of distant galaxies and nebulae. Her diary entries from this period are a blend of artistic analysis and scientific observation, revealing the deep connections between the visual and the astronomical. Lydia's fascination with these intersections fueled her passion for sharing the beauty of the universe with others.

Through her study of celestial art, Lydia discovered the power of creativity to illuminate the mysteries of the cosmos. She saw the stars and planets as a source of inspiration for artists, drawing connections between the rhythms of the universe and the patterns of artistic expression. Her diary became a repository of these reflections, filled with detailed notes and poetic passages that celebrated the beauty and complexity of the universe. Lydia's work in celestial art was a testament to the interconnectedness of all things, revealing the profound impact of the cosmos on human creativity.

10

Chapter 10: The Philosophy of the Stars

Lydia's journey through the cosmos was not just a scientific and artistic endeavor; it was also a philosophical exploration. She began to delve into the ways in which the universe influenced human thought and belief, drawing connections between the cosmos and the great philosophical questions of existence. Her diary entries from this period are a blend of philosophical inquiry and scientific observation, revealing the deep connections between the celestial and the philosophical.

One of Lydia's most profound insights came from her study of the concept of infinity. She marveled at the vastness of the universe, contemplating the endless expanse of space and the mysteries it held. Her diary became a space for her to document her reflections on infinity, filled with detailed notes and poetic passages that captured the awe and wonder of the cosmos. Lydia's insights highlighted the power of the universe to inspire deep philosophical contemplation.

Lydia's exploration of the philosophy of the stars also led her to consider the ways in which the cosmos influenced human belief systems. She observed the ways in which different cultures had interpreted the night sky, drawing connections between celestial phenomena and religious and spiritual beliefs. Her diary entries from this period are a blend of anthropological observation and philosophical reflection, revealing the deep connections between the celestial and the cultural. Lydia's work in this area opened new pathways for understanding the interplay between the cosmos and human thought.

Through her exploration of the philosophy of the stars, Lydia discovered the power of the cosmos to inspire a sense of wonder and connectedness. She saw the universe as a source of wisdom and insight, offering answers to the great philosophical questions of existence. Her diary became a repository of these reflections, filled with detailed notes and poetic passages that celebrated the beauty and complexity of the universe. Lydia's work in the philosophy of the stars was a testament to the interconnectedness of all things, revealing the profound impact of the cosmos on human thought and belief.

11

Chapter 11: The Intersection of Science and Spirituality

Lydia's journey through the cosmos led her to explore the intersection of science and spirituality.

She began to delve into the ways in which the universe influenced human understanding of the sacred, drawing connections between the cosmos and various spiritual beliefs. Her diary entries from this period are a blend of scientific observation and spiritual reflection, revealing the deep connections between the celestial and the divine.

Lydia's exploration of the intersection of science and spirituality led her to study the ways in which different cultures had interpreted the night sky. She discovered that many ancient civilizations had viewed celestial phenomena as manifestations of the divine, imbuing the stars and planets with spiritual significance. Her diary became a space for her to document these insights, filled with detailed notes and reflections on the ways in which the cosmos had shaped human spirituality. Lydia's work highlighted the enduring power of the universe to inspire a sense of wonder and reverence.

Through her study of the intersection of science and spirituality, Lydia also discovered the ways in which modern scientific discoveries had influenced contemporary spiritual beliefs. She observed how the awe-inspiring images captured by space telescopes had inspired a renewed sense of connectedness and transcendence among people of various faiths. Her diary entries from this period are a blend of scientific analysis and spiritual contemplation, revealing the deep connections between the exploration of the cosmos and the quest for meaning. Lydia's insights highlighted the power of the universe to foster a sense of unity and interconnectedness.

Lydia's work in the intersection of science and spirituality was a bridge between worlds, connecting the realms of scientific inquiry and spiritual exploration in new and profound ways. Her diary served as a space for her to document her discoveries and share her insights, inspiring a sense of wonder and curiosity that transcended disciplinary boundaries. Through her writing, Lydia fostered a holistic understanding of the cosmos, one that celebrated the beauty and complexity of the universe and its profound impact on human spirituality.

12

Chapter 12: The Legacy of the Stars

As Lydia's journey through the cosmos neared its culmination, she began to reflect on the legacy of her work. Her diary entries from this period are filled with introspective reflections on the impact of her discoveries and the ways in which she had contributed to the fields of astronomy, literature, psychology, and spirituality. Lydia's work had bridged the gap between these diverse disciplines, creating a holistic understanding of the universe and its profound influence on the human experience.

Lydia's reflections on her legacy led her to consider the ways in which her diary had served as a catalyst for exploration and discovery. She saw her writings as a testament to the power of curiosity and wonder, inspiring others to look to the stars and seek answers to the great questions of existence. Her diary became a repository of these reflections, filled with detailed notes and poetic passages that celebrated the beauty and complexity of the cosmos. Lydia's work highlighted the enduring power of the universe to inspire a sense of awe and reverence.

Through her reflections on her legacy, Lydia also discovered the ways in which her work had influenced the lives of others. She received letters from people around the world who had been inspired by her writings, sharing their own experiences of wonder and discovery. Her diary entries from this period are a testament to the profound impact of her work, filled with heartfelt messages of gratitude and admiration. Lydia's insights highlighted the power of the cosmos to foster a sense of connectedness and transcendence.

Lydia's journey through the cosmos had come full circle, from the dawn of discovery to the legacy of the stars. Her diary served as a bridge between worlds, connecting the realms of science, literature, psychology, and spirituality in new and profound ways. Through her writing, Lydia had fostered a holistic understanding of the cosmos, one that celebrated the beauty and complexity of the universe and its profound impact on the human experience. Her diary was a testament to the interconnectedness of all things, revealing the enduring power of the cosmos to inspire a sense of wonder and reverence.

13

Epilogue: A New Dawn

Lydia's journey through the cosmos had come to an end, but her legacy lived on. Her diary, a treasure trove of insights and reflections, continued to inspire new generations of explorers and dreamers. The pages of her diary had bridged the gap between science, literature, psychology, and spirituality, creating a holistic understanding of the universe and its profound influence on the human experience.

As the sun rose over Blue Haven, casting its golden light on the quiet town, Lydia's spirit lived on in the hearts of those who had been touched by her work. Her diary had become a beacon of hope and inspiration, a testament to the power of curiosity and wonder. Through her writings, Lydia had created a lasting legacy, one that celebrated the beauty and complexity of the cosmos and its profound impact on the human soul.

The Astronomer's Diary had become more than just a personal record of Lydia's thoughts and discoveries; it had become a bridge between worlds, connecting the realms of science, literature, psychology, and spirituality in new and profound ways. Through her writing, Lydia had fostered a holistic understanding of the cosmos, one that celebrated the interconnectedness of all things and the enduring power of the universe to inspire a sense of wonder and reverence.

And so, as the stars continued to shine in the night sky, Lydia's legacy lived on, a testament to the endless possibilities of exploration and discovery.

Her diary was a living testament to the interconnectedness of the cosmos and the human mind, revealing the profound impact of space on the human experience. Through her writings, Lydia had created a bridge between worlds, inspiring new generations to look to the stars and seek answers to the great questions of existence.

14

Chapter 13: The Rhythms of the Cosmos

Lydia's journey through the universe had always been guided by the rhythms of celestial bodies. She marveled at the regularity of planetary orbits and the predictable cycles of stars. Her diary entries from this period delve into the deeper meaning of these cosmic rhythms, drawing parallels with the rhythms of human life. Lydia found comfort in the predictable patterns of the universe, seeing them as a reflection of the natural order that governed all things.

Through her observations, Lydia discovered that the rhythms of the cosmos had a profound impact on human creativity and expression. She noted how the phases of the moon influenced artistic endeavors, with certain periods fostering a burst of creativity while others brought introspection. Her diary entries are rich with reflections on the ways in which celestial cycles mirrored the ebb and flow of human emotions and creativity. Lydia's insights highlighted the deep connections between the rhythms of the universe and the rhythms of life on Earth.

Lydia's work in this area also led her to explore the concept of cosmic resonance. She observed how certain frequencies and patterns in the universe resonated with the human mind, inspiring a sense of harmony and connectedness. Her diary became a repository of these reflections, filled with detailed notes and poetic passages that celebrated the beauty and complexity of cosmic resonance. Lydia's exploration of the rhythms of the cosmos was a testament to the interconnectedness of all things, revealing the profound impact of the universe on human thought and expression.

Through her study of the rhythms of the cosmos, Lydia discovered the power of the universe to inspire a sense of wonder and harmony. Her diary served as a space for her to document her findings and share her insights, fostering a deeper understanding of the interconnectedness of all things. Lydia's work in this area was a bridge between worlds, connecting the realms of science, art, and psychology in new and profound ways.

15

Chapter 14: The Universe Within

Lydia's journey through the cosmos had always been as much an inward exploration as an outward one. She saw the stars and planets as mirrors of the human mind, reflecting the vastness and complexity of the inner landscape. Her diary entries from this period delve into the psychological and philosophical implications of this interconnectedness, revealing the profound impact of the universe on the human psyche.

One of Lydia's most significant insights came from her exploration of the concept of the "universe within." She observed how the vastness of the cosmos mirrored the depths of the human mind, with both realms filled with mysteries and wonders waiting to be discovered. Her diary became a space for her to document these reflections, filled with detailed notes and poetic passages that celebrated the beauty and complexity of the inner landscape. Lydia's work in this area opened new pathways for understanding the connections between the cosmos and the mind.

Through her exploration of the universe within, Lydia also discovered the therapeutic potential of space-related experiences. She observed how the awe and wonder inspired by the cosmos could foster a sense of inner peace and connectedness, promoting psychological well-being. Her diary entries are filled with reflections on the ways in which celestial phenomena influenced mental health, highlighting the therapeutic power of the universe. Lydia's insights contributed to a deeper understanding of the psychological dimensions of space exploration.

Lydia's work in the universe within was a bridge between worlds, connecting the realms of psychology and astronomy in new and profound ways. Her diary served as a space for her to document her discoveries and share her insights, fostering a holistic understanding of the interconnectedness of all things. Through her writing, Lydia inspired others to look to the stars and explore the depths of their own minds, revealing the profound impact of the cosmos on the human experience.

16

Chapter 15: The Future of Exploration

As Lydia's journey through the cosmos drew to a close, she began to reflect on the future of space exploration. Her diary entries from this period are filled with visionary reflections on the possibilities that lay ahead, as humanity continued to reach for the stars. Lydia's work had always been guided by a sense of curiosity and wonder, and she saw the future of exploration as a continuation of this timeless quest for knowledge and understanding.

Through her reflections on the future of exploration, Lydia envisioned a world where space travel became more accessible, allowing people from all walks of life to experience the awe and wonder of the cosmos. She saw the potential for new discoveries and innovations that could transform the way humans understood the universe and their place within it. Her diary became a space for her to document these visionary ideas, filled with detailed notes and poetic passages that celebrated the possibilities of the future.

Lydia also considered the ethical implications of space exploration, reflecting on the responsibilities that came with venturing into the cosmos. She noted the importance of preserving the integrity of celestial bodies and respecting the potential for life beyond Earth. Her diary entries from this period are a testament to her thoughtful and conscientious approach to exploration, highlighting the need for a balanced and respectful relationship with the universe. Lydia's insights contributed to a deeper understanding of the ethical dimensions of space exploration.

Through her reflections on the future of exploration, Lydia fostered a sense of hope and inspiration for generations to come. Her diary served as a space for her to share her visionary ideas and insights, encouraging others to look to the stars with a sense of wonder and curiosity. Lydia's work in this area was a bridge between worlds, connecting the realms of science, ethics, and imagination in new and profound ways. Her legacy lived on, inspiring new generations of explorers to reach for the stars and seek answers to the great questions of existence.

Book Description:

The Astronomer's Diary, Bridging Literature, Psychology, and the Wonders of Space is a journey through the cosmos and the human soul, revealing the profound interconnectedness of all things. Through Lydia's diary, readers are invited to explore the beauty and complexity of the universe, the richness of human creativity, and the deep connections between science, art, psychology, and spirituality. This book is a testament to the enduring power of curiosity and wonder, inspiring a sense of reverence for the cosmos and the mysteries it holds.

The Astronomer's Diary, Bridging Literature, Psychology, and the Wonders of Space is an extraordinary exploration of the cosmos through the eyes of Dr. Lydia Marlow, a renowned astronomer. This captivating book seamlessly weaves together the realms of science, literature, psychology, and spirituality, offering readers a holistic understanding of the universe and its profound impact on the human experience. Through Lydia's diary entries, readers embark on a journey that delves into the mysteries of the cosmos, the beauty of poetic and artistic expressions inspired by the stars, and the psychological and philosophical implications of space exploration. *The Astronomer's Diary* is a testament to the interconnectedness of all things, revealing the enduring power of the universe to inspire awe, wonder, and a sense of reverence.

www.ingramcontent.com/pod-product-compliance
Lightning Source LLC
LaVergne TN
LVHW020501080526
838202LV00057B/6081